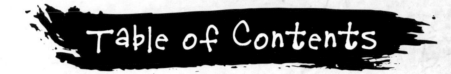

Table of Contents

Introduction

Hey! Welcome to the Best Quiz Ever series. This is a book. Duh. But it's also a pretty awesome quiz. Don't worry. It's not about math. Or history. Or anything you might get graded on. Snooze.

This is a quiz all about YOU.

To Take the Best Quiz Ever:

Answer honestly!
Keep track of your answers. But don't write in the book!
(Hint: Make a copy of this handy chart.)
Don't see the answer you want? Pick the closest one.
Take it alone. Take it with friends!
Have fun! Obviously.

Question 1 _____

Question 2 _____

Question 3 _____

Question 4 _____

Question 5 _____

Question 6 _____

Question 7 _____

Question 8 _____

Question 9 _____

Question 10 _____

Question 11 _____

Question 12 _____

To get a copy of this activity, visit
www.cherrylakepublishing.com/activities.

Question 1

Your best quality is that you are:

A. Friendly

B. Unique

C. Able to talk to anyone

D. Exciting

Did you know?
A tiger cub and a baby monkey became best friends at a zoo in China.

Your favorite season is:

A. Summer! Perfect for playing outside!

B. Winter! Everyone loves summer.

C. Spring! So many flowers!

D. Fall! I love the changing weather.

Did you know?

The year 1816 was "the year without a summer." A **volcano** made the weather cold all over the world.

You would love to ____, but your mom would never let you.

A. Go whitewater rafting with friends

B. Join a roller derby team

C. Try out for a reality show

D. Start a gossip vlog

Did you know?

The player who scores points on a roller derby team is called a jammer.

Choose a color:

A. Green

B. Black

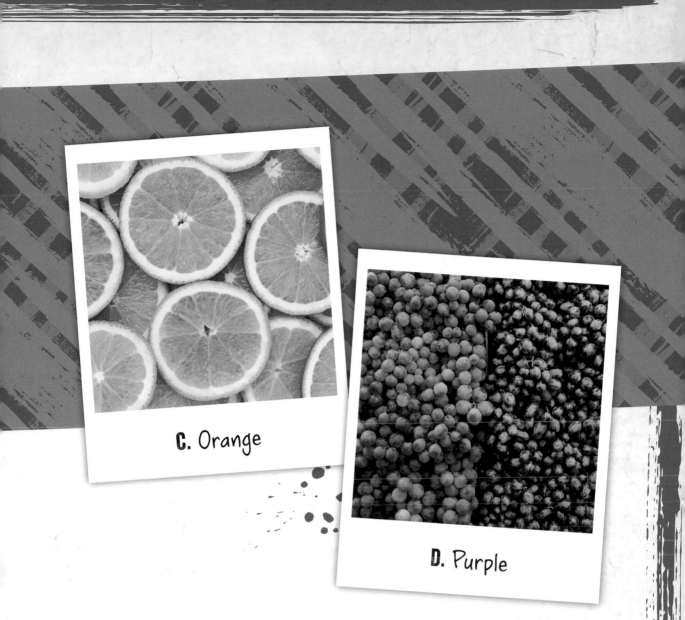

C. Orange

D. Purple

Did you know?
Orange is an important color in **Buddhism** and **Hinduism**. It symbolizes purity.

Your favorite movies are ones that:

A. I will laugh at

B. Will scare me

C. Have the latest heartthrob

D. Will make me cry

Did you know?

Scream *is a series of scary movies by Kevin Williamson and Wes Craven. They were released between 1996 and 2011.*

You're stranded on a desert island. You would kill for:

A. A buddy

B. Some tunes

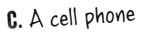

C. A cell phone

D. A beach towel and sunglasses

Did you know?

José Salvador Alvarenga was **stranded** at sea on a small fishing boat for 13 months. He survived on raw fish and turtle blood.

When the Olympics are on, you are:

A. Glued to the TV!

B. Not watching the Olympics

C. Judging the outfits

D. Waiting for gymnastics or figure skating

Did you know?

In the 2014 Winter Olympics, Americans Meryl Davis and Charlie White were ice dancing champions.

Pick one:

A. Mountains

B. Desert

C. City

D. Ocean

Did you know?

Antarctica may be cold, but it is the world's biggest desert. It almost never gets precipitation.

Question 9

The coolest birthday party would be:

A. A day at an amusement park with friends

B. Party? I'd rather just have the new Xbox.

22

C. Cake and a bounce house with all my friends

D. Mani/pedis and a sleepover with my besties

Did you know?

High school students in Alabama set a record for longest time in a bounce house. They jumped for 25 hours, 25 minutes, and 25 seconds!

Your dream job is:

A. Pro athlete

B. Hacker

C. Talk show host

D. Movie star

Did you know?
Soccer player Cristiano Ronaldo makes $80 million a year.

You realize you left the textbook you need to do your homework at school. You:

A. Call a friend to borrow hers

B. Do nothing. Homework is overrated.

C. Do the homework with a friend before class

D. Make Mom drive me back to school

Did you know?
Gaithersburg Elementary School in Rockville, Maryland, has a "no homework" policy.

On the Fourth of July, you're usually:

A. Waiting for the fireworks!

B. Inside in the air-conditioning

C. In the parade

D. At the beach

Did you know?

The Guinness World Record for the largest fireworks display is 540,382 fireworks set off by Svea Fyrverkerier, a business in Norway.

You're done! Now you tally your score. Add up your As, Bs, Cs, and Ds. What letter do you have the most of? BTW, if you have a tie, you're a little bit of both.

As: Dog

You're a dog person. You love to play outside with a ball and lots of friends. Movie nights and sleepovers are also fun! You always look on the bright side. People like to be around you. People have said that you're "a real charmer." You would love to have a furry friend to play outside or veg on the couch with.

Bs: Snake

You march to the beat of a different drummer. You love being a little different from your friends. Some people think you're shy. But you just don't want to waste your time on people you don't like. You like to know about cool music or shows before anyone else. And you have your own fashion sense. Even if it is usually black. A snake would be a perfect pet for you!

Cs: Bird

Your friends might call you a chatterbox. And your teachers would for sure call you a chatterbox! You just have so much to say! You like to be loud when you talk or sing. And even in the way you dress—bright colors all the way! Your bubbly personality commands attention. You should think about a colorful, feathered friend as a pet. And you can teach him to talk, too. Bonus!

Ds: Cat

Cats can be quiet and moody. Or silly and playful. Just like you! You never know what you are going to be in the mood for. You are careful about choosing your friends. And it can take you time to warm up to others. But when you are with a good friend or two, you love to relax and be silly. You would get along with a cat perfectly!

Glossary

Buddhism (BOO-diz-uhm) a religion based on the teachings of Buddha

hacker (HAK-ur) someone who has a special skill for getting into a computer system without permission

Hinduism (HIN-doo-iz-uhm) a religion and philosophy practiced mainly in India

stranded (STRAND-id) left in a strange or unpleasant place, especially without any money or any way to depart

volcano (vahl-KAY-noh) a mountain with openings through which molten lava, ash, and hot gases erupt, sometimes violently

Index